ADVENT+CHRISTMASTIDE 2016

I0388767

YOUR VITAL STATS

NAME

BIRTHDAY   **BAPTISM DAY**

PATRON SAINT   **HOME CHURCH**

MOTTO

MISSION:CHRISTIAN
A JOURNAL FOR YOUNG CATHOLICS ON A MISSION

USING YOUR MISSION JOURNAL DAY BY DAY

1. GET BRIEFED WITH GOD'S WORD

Each entry in the M:C journal suggests a reading for the day. You'll need to look up the reading in a Bible. If you can, use a copy of the New American Bible: Revised Edition. It's the translation that U.S. Catholics use at Mass, and it has handy footnoes that will help you understand the reading.

2. MEET YOUR MENTOR

After you have (slowly and prayerfully) read the Bible reading for the day, check out the saint (or blessed, or venerable) whose feast the Church celebrates on that day. These are people the whole Church holds up as models of how to live the Christian life, and they can be mentors—teachers and guides—as you carry out your mission.

3. PRAY

Prayer is about spending time in relationship with God. It is essential to the success of your mission, because it is through prayer that God teaches us, encourages us, and gives us the help we need throughout the day. Write down your prayer in your M:C journal. Writing your prayer will help you be specific, and you can check back on what you prayed for at the end of the day.

4. GET YOUR MISSION

Each day, your M:C journal will suggest a mission, using the day's Bible reading or saint as an inspiration. The mission might be a specific task, or it might be very general—for example, "Feed someone who is hungry." In the last case, you will need to figure out (with the help of the Holy Spirit) what that mission will look like. It might mean donating money to a charity, or it might mean getting a snack for your younger brother . . . or something else.

5. REPORT

At the end of the day, come back to your journal to complete your "mission report." Were you able to complete your mission? If not, what prevented you? If so, how did it go? Describe what happened, and how you felt. What can you learn about yourself from your experience? How was God present to you in your experience?

The best place to begin? Use the prayer on the next page to pray for your missions!

A PRAYER FOR MISSION

God knows me and calls me by name.
He has not created me for nothing;
somehow I am necessary for his purposes.
He has created me to do something or to be something
for which no one else is created.
I have my mission—I never may know it in this life,
but I shall be told it in the next.

Therefore, I will trust Him.
If I am in sickness, my sickness may serve Him;
in perplexity, my perplexity may serve Him;
if I am in sorrow, my sorrow may serve Him.
He may prolong my life, or shorten it;
He knows what He is about.
He may take away my friends,
or throw me among strangers;
still He knows what He is about.
Let me be Your blind instrument, Lord.
I ask not to see; I ask not to know;
I ask simply to be used.

—adapted from a meditation by St. John Henry Newman

POPE FRANCIS
WORDS FOR MISSION

DEAR YOUNG PEOPLE . . . JESUS IS WAITING FOR YOU. He has confidence in you and is counting on you! He has so many things to say to each of you. . . . Do not be afraid to look into his eyes, full of infinite love for you. Open yourselves to his merciful gaze, so ready to forgive all your sins. A look from him can change your lives and heal the wounds of your souls. His eyes can quench the thirst that dwells deep in your young hearts, a thirst for love, for peace, for joy and for true happiness. Come to Him and do not be afraid!

Come to him and say from the depths of your hearts: "Jesus, I trust in You!" Let yourselves be touched by his boundless mercy, so that in turn you may become apostles of mercy by your actions, words and prayers in our world, wounded by selfishness, hatred and so much despair.

Carry with you the flame of Christ's merciful love in every sphere of your daily life and to the very ends of the earth. In this mission, I am with you with my encouragement and prayers.

MESSAGE FOR WORLD YOUTH DAY 2016

A THANKSGIVING GRATITUDE JOURNAL

IN THE DAYS leading up to Thanksgiving, keep a Gratitude Journal, listing one thing you are thankful for every day. Bring your gratitude list to your family's Thanksgiving meal to display or to share during your family's meal prayer.

AN ADVENT CHECKLIST

Stores start displaying Christmas decorations sometime in mid-autumn, but for the Church, Christmas doesn't begin until sunset on December 24. In the weeks before Christmas, however, Christians observe the season of Advent. The word *Advent* comes from the Latin *adventus*, which means a coming or arrival. It is a time for turning away from sin and preparing for the coming of the Savior.

During Advent, Christians prepare for Christ's coming by remembering the long years during which Israel waited for the coming of the Messiah, and by looking forward to the final coming of Christ at the end of time. It is also a time to prepare our hearts for the coming of Christ here and now.

Here are some ways you can observe Advent in your family. Put a checkmark by each thing you plan to do for Advent.

- ☐ **Get an Advent wreath.** If your family doesn't have an Advent wreath, get one or make one, and then use it to have a little Advent prayer service at least once a week.

- ☐ **Make up an Advent list.** When you make up your Christmas list, make up your Advent list, too. Put on your list all the spiritual gifts you would like to receive in honor of Jesus' birthday, or items you would like donated to charity in your name.

- ☐ **Learn all the verses of "O Come, O Come Emmanuel."** This ancient Advent hymn uses language and images from the Old Testament to anticipate the coming of Emmanuel (a Greek word meaning "God is with us" and a title of Christ).

- ☐ **Wait to put up Christmas decorations.** Advent is about waiting for the birth of Christ, so putting Christmas decorations up right away doesn't quite fit with the spirit of the season. Instead, your family might add just a few lights and decorations each Sunday of Advent (to mirror the lighting of the candles on the Advent wreath).

- ☐ **Make a Jesse Tree.** A Jesse Tree is a tree decorated with ornaments based on symbols of Old Testament events preparing for the coming of Christ. Different people use different symbols; you can find suggestions online.

- ☐ **Bless your Nativity scene.** If you have a Christmas manger or Nativity scene, leave the baby Jesus out until Christmas Eve. Your family may wish to bless it; search for "Blessing of a Christmas Manger or Nativity Scene" online. M:C

This Tree of Jesse icon reminds us that God prepared his people for the coming of the Christ.
Tilemahos Efthimiadis (1666)

THURSDAY, NOVEMBER 24

YOUR PRAYER
What do you want to say to God today?

YOUR MISSION

Go back to your Gratitude Journal (page 4) and fill in as many blank spaces as possible. Read or post your list as part of your family's Thanksgiving celebration.

YOUR MISSION REPORT
Did you complete your mission? How did it go?

Give thanks to God

THANKSGIVING

Today we give thanks to God for the many blessings in our lives, imitating the meal the Pilgrims held in 1621. But did you know the very first Thanksgiving on American soil was celebrated on September 8, 1565 in St. Augustine, Florida, when the Spanish settlers held a feast and Mass with the local Native Americans? Here's anther fun fact: Squanto, the Patuxet Indian who helped the Pilgrims, was Catholic. He had been captured by English settlers and sold into slavery in Spain, where he was freed by Franciscan friars and baptized.

TODAY'S READING
Luke 17:11-19

Only one of ten men whom Jesus heals of leprosy returns to thank him. What do you thank Jesus for today?

This is also the feast day of Sts. Andrew Dũng-Lạc, Pierre Dumoulin-Borie, and other Vietnamese martyrs.

The earth and the sky fled

FRIDAY, NOVEMBER 25

TODAY'S READING

Revelation 20:1-4, 11—21:2

After the dragon is tied up, all the dead are gathered before God to be judged, and a new heaven and earth replace the old. How does God's victory over sin and death affect you?

TODAY'S SAINT

St. Catherine of Alexandria (c. 310)
Catherine was an 18-year-old convert to Christianity who turned down the emperor's offer to spare her life if only she would marry him. He sent his best philosophers to persuade her to give up her faith; instead, she persuaded them to become Christian. Much of her story is legendary, based on the lives of several young martyrs.

YOUR PRAYER
What do you want to say to God today?

YOUR MISSION

Celebrate a "Reverse Black Friday" by going through your home and selecting things to give away.*

YOUR MISSION REPORT
Did you complete your mission? How did it go?

---

* Bonus mission: Today is International Buy Nothing Day: Instead of shopping, rebel against consumerism by doing random acts of kindness (www.buynothingday.co.uk)

SATURDAY, NOVEMBER 26

God shall give them light

YOUR PRAYER
What do you want to say to God today?

TODAY'S READINGS

Revelation 22:1-7
John sees a vision of heaven that is full of symbolism; compare it to the vision described by the prophet Ezekiel in the reading for November 9 (see Ezekiel 47:1-2, 8-9, 12).

TODAY'S SAINT

Fr. James Alberione
(1884-1971)

After praying for four hours before the Blessed Sacrament, Fr. Alberione felt called to preach the Gospel to all peoples in the spirit of the Apostle Paul. He did this by publishing popular books, pamphlets, magazines, and newspapers. Today, the communities he founded—the Society of St. Paul and the Daughters of St. Paul—continue his evangelizing work by producing all sorts of Catholic media.

"I felt deeply obliged to prepare myself to do something for God and the men of the new century in which I would live."

YOUR MISSION

Like Father James Alberione, pray before the Blessed Sacrament to know what God would have you do for the world.

YOUR MISSION REPORT
Did you complete your mission? How did it go?

November 26, 1863: President Abraham Lincoln establishes Thanksgiving as an annual celebration.

Walk in the light

SUNDAY, NOVEMBER 27

FIRST SUNDAY OF ADVENT

Advent begins today! See page 71 for more about Advent. Light the first purple candle on your Advent wreath today and this week.

TODAY'S READINGS

Isaiah 2:1-5
O house of Jacob, come, let us walk in the light of the Lord!

Romans 13:11-14
Let us then throw off the works of darkness and put on the armor of light.

Matthew 24:37-44
Therefore, stay awake! For you do not know on which day your Lord will come.

Advent is all about waiting for the coming of Jesus. In the readings from the Old Testament, we remember how Israel waited for the coming of the Messiah; we prepare for his coming into our lives today; and we reflect on his coming at the end of time. How will you prepare for Christ's coming this Advent?

YOUR PRAYER

What do you want to say to God today?

YOUR MISSION

On this first Sunday of Advent, imagine that Jesus is going to show up at your home "in the flesh." Prepare your house and your bedroom (and your heart!) by decorating with things to welcome him, and getting rid of anything you would not want him to see.

YOUR MISSION REPORT

Did you complete your mission? How did it go?

Happy New Year! Today marks the first day of the new Church year, during which all the Sunday readings will come from Year A, and all the weekday readings will come from Cycle 1.

MONDAY, NOVEMBER 28

YOUR PRAYER
What do you want to say to God today?

YOUR MISSION

Imitating the great faith of the Roman centurion in today's Gospel, ask Jesus for something big today.

YOUR MISSION REPORT
Did you complete your mission? How did it go?

I will come

TODAY'S READING
Matthew 8:5-11
A Roman centurion (commander of one hundred soldiers) asks Jesus to heal his servant—but in a way that demonstrates great faith. We repeat his words to Jesus at every Mass.

TODAY'S SAINT
St. James of the Marche
(1394-1476)
The Franciscan friar who preached to hundreds of thousands across Europe, promoting the Holy Name of Jesus and performing miracles. To help the poor, he established places where they could get low-interest loans on pawned items.

"Beloved and most holy word of God! . . . You make the wretched holy, and men of earth citizens of heaven."

November 28, 1981: Our Lady of Kibeho first appears to schoolchildren in Kibeho, Rwanda.

A bud shall blossom

TUESDAY, NOVEMBER 29

TODAY'S READING

Isaiah 11:1-10

The prophet Isaiah offers a beautiful vision of the Messiah and the reign of peace and justice he brings. What is your vision of peace?

TODAY'S SAINT

Servant of God Dorothy Day (1897-1980)
Dorothy Day was a journalist and social justice activist who worked for votes for women, workers' rights, and an end to war and poverty. The birth of her daughter led to her baptism in the Catholic Church. After praying for a way to continue her work as a lay Catholic, she and Peter Maurin started the Catholic Worker movement.

"We have all known the long loneliness and we have learned that the only solution is love, and that love comes with community."

YOUR PRAYER

What do you want to say to God today?

YOUR MISSION

A central value of the Catholic Worker movement is hospitality—that is, welcoming each person as a special guest, or even an "ambassador of God." Your mission: Like Dorothy and Peter, offer hospitality to someone who is lonely or in need of welcome.*

YOUR MISSION REPORT

Did you complete your mission? How did it go?

* Bonus mission: It's the National Day of Giving: Find a way to give to your community! #GivingTuesday

WEDNESDAY, NOVEMBER 30

YOUR PRAYER
What do you want to say to God today?

They left their nets

TODAY'S READING
Matthew 4:18-22
Peter and his brother Andrew are hard at work fishing when Jesus calls them to follow him. What would you do if you were Andrew?

TODAY'S SAINT
St. Andrew
Originally a disciple of John the Baptist, Andrew began following Jesus at John's urging. There are many legends about what Andrew did after the resurrection of Jesus; many say he preached the Gospel in the eastern part of the Roman Empire. Tradition says he was martyred by crucifixion.

"We have found the Messiah."

YOUR MISSION

Like St. Andrew, announce the Good News to the whole world (starting at home!). Your mission: Make plans with friends or family to go Christmas caroling during the Advent or Christmas season. Have an adult help you contact local nursing homes, hospitals, shelters, and jails.*

YOUR MISSION REPORT
Did you complete your mission? How did it go?

* Bonus mission: On this International Cities for Life Day, organized by the Community of Sant'Egidio, join cities around the world and the Church in working for an end to the death penalty.

Set solidly on rock

TODAY'S READING

Matthew 7:21, 24-27

Building a house on sand is way easier and faster than building on rock, but Jesus says we should build to last any kind of weather. What is *your* foundation?

TODAY'S SAINT

Blessed Charles de Foucauld (1858-1916)
As a young man, Charles rejected his Catholic faith in favor of a life of adventure. The Jews and Muslims he met during his exploration of Morocco inspired him to take up his faith again; he became a Trappist monk and lived in the Algerian desert offering hospitality to travelers of every religion. His writings and way of life inspired countless others to imitate him.

"There is, I believe, no word from the Gospel that has a more profound impression on me nor has transformed my life more than this: 'Whatever you do for the least of my brothers, you do for me.'"

THURSDAY, DECEMBER 1

YOUR PRAYER
What do you want to say to God today?

YOUR MISSION

Working from today's Gospel and the spirituality of Blessed Charles de Foucauld, help provide safe shelter for someone.*

YOUR MISSION REPORT
Did you complete your mission? How did it go?

* Bonus mission: World AIDS Day: Search "World AIDS Day U.S. Catholic bishops" for ways to act.

FRIDAY, DECEMBER 2

Their eyes were opened

YOUR PRAYER
What do you want to say to God today?

TODAY'S READING
Matthew 9:27-31

Two blind men ask for Jesus to heal them, but Jesus asks them a question first: "Do you believe I can do this?" Why is faith so important when Jesus heals people?

TODAY'S SAINT
Blessed Liduina Meneguzzi
(1901-1941)

Sister Liduina was sent as a missionary to Dire-Dawa in Ethiopia in 1937. There, she worked in the local hospital. When the hospital was bombed during World War II, her courage and selflessness in rescuing and caring for the wounded and dying earned her the respect of both the soldiers and the natives.

YOUR MISSION

Like Sister Liduina, spread cheer today. Get some wrapped candies or fresh flowers and distribute them to people in a grocery store, school, nursing home, or church...along with a smile and a word of blessing!*

YOUR MISSION REPORT
Did you complete your mission? How did it go?

GOD'S CREATION
CHRISTMAS BIRD COUNT

If you like to watch and count birds, then plan to register for the Audubon Society's annual Christmas Bird Count, December 14–January 5. Learn more at audubon.org.

* Bonus mission: On this International Day for the Abolition of Slavery, get educated about human trafficking.

He gave them authority

SATURDAY, DECEMBER 3

TODAY'S READING

Matthew 9:35-10:1, 5, 6-8
Moved by pity for the people, Jesus sends the Twelve on a special mission. Do you see people today who are "troubled and abandoned"?

TODAY'S SAINT

St. Francis Xavier
(1506-1552)
Francis Xavier was one of the founding members of the Society of Jesus (Jesuits). He was sent on missions all over Asia, including India, Japan, and Malaysia. Wherever he went, he lived with the poor and tried to learn the local language and customs; he even adopted Japanese dress to better fit in with the people.

"In this way I go all round the country, bringing the natives into the fold of Jesus Christ, and the joy that I feel in this is far too great to be expressed."

YOUR PRAYER
What do you want to say to God today?

YOUR MISSION

St. Francis Xavier used to make up little songs to help children learn the Catholic faith. Your mission: Make up a little song with an important message about the faith, and sing it for someone (maybe a younger child?).*

YOUR MISSION REPORT
Did you complete your mission? How did it go?

*Bonus mission: On this International Day of Persons with Disabilities, find out how you can help.

SUNDAY, DECEMBER 4

The root of Jesse

YOUR PRAYER
What do you want to say to God today?

SECOND SUNDAY OF ADVENT
Light two purple candles on your Advent wreath today and throughout this week.

TODAY'S READINGS

Isaiah 11:1-10
On that day, the root of Jesse, set up as a signal for the nations, the Gentiles shall seek out, for his dwelling shall be glorious.

Romans 15:4-9
Welcome one another, then, as Christ welcomed you, for the glory of God.

Matthew 3:1-12
He will baptize you with the Holy Spirit and fire.

YOUR MISSION
On this second Sunday of Advent, "produce good fruit" (Matthew 3:8) by collecting fruit (canned or dried) to give to your local food shelf or food drive.

ISAIAH THE PROPHET
We hear from the prophet Isaiah *a lot* during Advent, especially the joyful parts in which he paints a picture of what God's salvation will look like. What does Isaiah include in his vision? How do you picture God's salvation?

YOUR MISSION REPORT
Did you complete your mission? How did it go?

Today is *Eid il-Burbara*, or Saint Barbara's Day, among Middle Eastern Christians in Lebanon, Syria, Jordan, Palestine and Turkey; the holiday resembles Halloween, with kids going door to door for treats.

The desert shall bloom

MONDAY, DECEMBER 5

TODAY'S READING

Isaiah 35:1-10
Isaiah paints a picture of what God's salvation will look like, both for his people and all of creation. How would you picture God's salvation?

TODAY'S SAINT

St. Sabas (b. 439)
The boy who sought refuge in a monastery to escape abuse at home. He loved life as a monk, but at age 18 he left to seek a life of solitude and prayer in a cave near Jerusalem. Over the years, others joined him, until a monastic community grew up in the place; it is still there today, and Sabas is regarded as one of the founders of eastern monasticism.

"We must resist the devils, but yield to men for the sake of peace."

YOUR PRAYER
What do you want to say to God today?

YOUR MISSION

Imitate St. Sabas by finding a cave in which you can fast and pray. (Your "cave" might have to be a snow cave, or your closet, or a blanket cave... be creative!)

YOUR MISSION REPORT
Did you complete your mission? How did it go?

International Day of the Ninja: Dress like a ninja today!

St. Nicholas
Bishop of Myra
270-343

An Advent Prayer to St. Nicholas

St. Nicholas,
pray for me this Advent:
that like you, I might be
a help to those in need;
a rescuer of those in peril;
a rock opposing the enemy;
a light in the storm;
a lover of justice;
and a zealous friend
of Christ.

Amen.

MEET
ST. NICHOLAS

LIVED: Nicholas was born to wealthy Greek parents in the year 270 on the coast of what is now Turkey. He died on December 6, 343, in Myra, where he was bishop.

MISSION: As bishop of Myra, Nicholas devoted himself to caring for the poor and defending children. At the Council of Nicea, he defended the divinity of Christ.

ADVENTURES: The man who would later become the basis for our modern-day "Santa Claus" was gentle with children, but tough when it came to defending truth and justice. During the persecution of Christians, Bishop Nicholas was thrown in prison and tortured. Scientists studying his skull have found his nose had been broken, probably by Roman soldiers during the bishop's time in prison.

As a young man, Nicholas made a pilgrimage to the Holy Land so he could pray at the places Jesus lived. During the voyage, a fierce storm struck the ship. "Do not fear; God will protect us," Nicholas told the sailors. Then he calmly prayed as the storm raged.

Finally, the storm calmed down, but not before a sailor fell from the rigging. Nicholas prayed over the seemingly dead man, who miraculously arose as if he had only been asleep.

Another time Bishop Nicholas learned of three sisters who wanted to marry, but were unable to afford a dowry. Nicholas visited the family's home in the middle of the night, throwing a small bag of gold coins in the window. The coins landed in a pair of shoes that were drying by the fire. Nicholas did this three times, supplying enough money for all the girls to marry.

When famine struck Myra in 312 and 313, Nicholas prayed to God for help. Soon he learned of several ships that had landed nearby, laden with grain destined for Egypt. He rushed to the port and begged the captain to sell some of the grain, promising the man that he would not get in trouble for the missing amount. Very reluctantly, the captain sold some of the grain to the people of Myra.

When the grain was unloaded in Egypt, true to the good bishop's word, it weighed as much as when it had been loaded! Back in Myra, the grain was enough to feed people for two years, with enough left over for planting. It was a miracle of sharing—the sort of miracle that is especially appropriate during Advent! **M:C**

TUESDAY, DECEMBER 6

He rejoices

YOUR PRAYER
What do you want to say to God today?

YOUR MISSION
Help someone find something they have lost. If you don't know anyone who needs that help today, search your home for things that have been lost: check under the couch, in cracks, outside, etc. Reflect: What does it mean to find someone who has been "lost" from the Church?*

YOUR MISSION REPORT
Did you complete your mission? How did it go?

FEAST OF ST. NICHOLAS
On the feast of St. Nicholas, children leave their shoes by the door for St. Nicholas to fill with candy (often foil-wrapped chocolate coins).

TODAY'S READING
Matthew 18:12-14
Go out and find those who are "lost" to God, Jesus tells his disciples. Who is "lost to God" in your world?

TODAY'S SAINT
St. Nicholas (270-343)
St. Nicholas was the bishop of Myra who once stopped the unjust execution of three men. He grabbed the executioner's sword out of his hands, unchained the men, and brought them back to the judge to demand their pardon.

"I am Nicholas, a sinner, servant of God, and bishop of Myra."

---

* Bonus mission: Organize a St. Nicholas party for younger kids: Don't forget the tradition of leaving shoes out for the visit of St. Nicholas! Leave coins, candies, or notes in each shoe.

I will give you rest

WEDNESDAY, DECEMBER 7

TODAY'S READING

Matthew 11:28-30
A yoke is a wooden bar that goes across the shoulders of an animal or person to help them carry or drag a heavy load. Jesus says that if we find our "yoke" to be heavy, we should let him do the work in us, In your prayer, ask Jesus to "work" in you today!

TODAY'S SAINT

St. Ambrose (340-397)
The bishop who defied the emperor, composed new hymns, developed Christian doctrine, and converted St. Augustine. He started out as a Roman governor. When a riot threatened to break out over who should be the next bishop, he went to the church to calm the mob. To his shock, the mob elected *him* their bishop—even though he wasn't even baptized!

"I will never betray the church of Christ. . . . I will die at the foot of the altar rather than desert it."

YOUR PRAYER
What do you want to say to God today?

YOUR MISSION
Make someone else's burden easier by helping them out today.

YOUR MISSION REPORT
Did you complete your mission? How did it go?

December 7, 1941: Japanese attack on Pearl Harbor launches the United States into World War II.

THURSDAY, DECEMBER 8

YOUR PRAYER
What do you want to say to God today?

YOUR MISSION

Go to Mass with your family today! It's a "holy day of obligation," which means the Church calls all the faithful to come together to celebrate.

Bonus mission: Set a date (maybe even today) to celebrate the sacrament of Penance this Advent so that you can have an "immaculate" heart for Christmas.

YOUR MISSION REPORT
Did you complete your mission? How did it go?

The Lord is with you

SOLEMNITY OF THE IMMACULATE CONCEPTION

On the Solemnity of the Immaculate Conception, we celebrate the immaculate ("stainless") conception of the Blessed Virgin Mary. That means that Mary was free of original sin from the moment Mary's mother, Anne, became pregnant with her. (This day is *not* about Mary's miraculous conception of Jesus!) That made her the perfect mother for Jesus, the holy Son of God, who came to take away all sin.

TODAY'S READING

Luke 1:26-38
The angel Gabriel announces to Mary that she will bear the Son of God. What is the very first thing Gabriel says about Mary? (Hint: It relates to today's feast!)

December 8, 1854: Pope Pius IX issues *Ineffabilis Deus*, declaring the doctrine of the Immaculate Conception,

Wisdom is vindicated

TODAY'S READING

Matthew 11:16-19
Jesus' critics won't be satisfied, no matter what he does. Jesus' closest followers will have the same experience. What is a good way of handling people who are never satisfied?

TODAY'S SAINT

St. Juan Diego (1474-1548) The humble Mexican Indian to whom the Virgin of Guadalupe appeared on this date in 1531. She spoke to him in Nahuatl, his native language, saying, "Juanito, my son, where are you going?"

GOD'S CREATION WATCH FOR...

In early winter, watch for the courtship calls of the Great Horned Owl; the Northern Lights; winter constellations (Orion, Cassiopeia, Pleiads).

FRIDAY, DECEMBER 9

YOUR PRAYER
What do you want to say to God today?

YOUR MISSION

Like Juan Diego, go to your bishop with "roses." Send your bishop a card or personal note. You can keep it simple (offer holiday greetings to cheer him up), or you can tell him about your encounter with Jesus, or share with him an important message.

YOUR MISSION REPORT
Did you complete your mission? How did it go?

Today is Anna's Day in Sweden: Begin preparing your lutefisk for Christmas Eve!

SATURDAY, DECEMBER 10

Elijah will indeed come

YOUR PRAYER
What do you want to say to God today?

_____
_____
_____
_____
_____

YOUR MISSION

Like Bernard, be ready to return all you have to God. Go through your things and choose several to donate to your local thrift shop; look especially for things that someone might like for Christmas.

YOUR MISSION REPORT
Did you complete your mission? How did it go?

_____
_____
_____
_____
_____

TODAY'S READING

Matthew 17:9, 10-13

Coming down the mountain after the Transfiguration (in which Moses and Elijah appear with Jesus), the disciples ask why Elijah must come before the Messiah. Jesus answers that Elijah has already come (in John the Baptist), which means the Messiah is on his way. For more about Elijah, see the first reading, Sirach 48:1-4, 9-11.

TODAY'S SAINT

Servant of God Bernard of Quintavalle
(d. 1241)

A wealthy and influential citizen of Assisi, Bernard was the first to join St. Francis, giving away all his wealth to do so. He was one of St. Francis's most trusted companions.

"I know that everything I have was given to me by God and on your advice I am now ready to return all to Him."

December 10, 1968: Death of Thomas Merton, the world-famous Trappist monk who once said, "There is no way of telling people that they are all shining like the sun. . . . The gate of heaven is everywhere."

Joy and gladness

SUNDAY, DECEMBER 11

THIRD SUNDAY IN ADVENT

Light three candles on your Advent wreath: two purple, and one rose.

GAUDETE SUNDAY

The third Sunday of Advent is Gaudete Sunday. The Latin word *Gaudete* means "rejoice," and that is what we do on this day: We rejoice because we are more than halfway through Advent, and the coming of Christ is near. We light the rose-colored candle on the Advent wreath rather than a purple one as a sign that we are taking a brief break from doing penance.

TODAY'S READINGS

Isaiah 35:1-6, 10
. . . they will meet with joy and gladness, sorrow and mourning will flee.

James 5:7-10
Be patient, brothers and sisters, until the coming of the Lord.

Matthew 11:2-11
. . . the dead are raised, and the poor have the good news proclaimed to them.

YOUR PRAYER
What do you want to say to God today?

YOUR MISSION

On this Guadete Sunday, spread joy and gladness to the people who need it most. Reflect: What is your favorite way of spreading joy and gladness?*

YOUR MISSION REPORT
Did you complete your mission? How did it go?

---

* Bonus mission: For Worldwide Candle Lighting Day, light a candle in memory of a child who has died.

MONDAY, DECEMBER 12

YOUR PRAYER
What do you want to say to God today?

YOUR MISSION

If Mary just wanted to have a church built, she could have appeared to the bishop! Instead, she appeared to Juan Diego to inspire his people, who often suffered under Spanish rule. Your mission: Learn about another culture so you can better reach out in friendship. Explore catholicsandcultures.org for a look at how different cultures practice the Catholic faith.

YOUR MISSION REPORT
Did you complete your mission? How did it go?

With the moon under her feet

FEAST OF OUR LADY OF GUADALUPE

On the morning of December 9, 1531, the Virgin Mary appeared to Juan Diego, identifying herself as the "mother of the very true deity" and asking for a church to be built there. Juan convinced skeptical Church authorities of the truth of the message by producing an armful of out-of-season roses from the folds of his garment; an image of the Virgin Mary as a young, pregnant native woman appeared on the garment as well. The image draws millions of pilgrims every year.

TODAY'S READING

Revelation 11:19; 12:1-6, 10
A great sign appeared in the sky, a woman clothed with the sun, with the moon under her feet, and on her head a crown of twelve stars.

December 12, 1917: Servant of God Father Edward J. Flanagan founds Boys Town as a farm village for wayward boys.

You did not believe him

TUESDAY, DECEMBER 13

TODAY'S READING

Matthew 21:28-32

Have you ever refused to do a chore for your parents? If so, you might just relate to this reading! What matters more to Jesus, words or actions?

TODAY'S SAINT

St. Lucia of Syracuse (d. 304) St. Lucia (Lucy) was a young Christian martyr. Later stories of her martyrdom included a one about her eyes getting gouged out, which led to the celebration of her feast as a festival of light. In Scandinavian cultures, a young girl dressed in a white dress and a red sash (the symbol of martyrdom) carries palms and wears a crown or wreath of candles on her head as she carries rolls or cookies and songs are sung.

YOUR PRAYER

What do you want to say to God today?

YOUR MISSION

In today's Gospel, Jesus wants our actions to reflect our words—especially when it comes to doing what the "father" (God) wants us to do. Your mission: Do what your father (and mother, and God!) wants you to do, with alacrity.

YOUR MISSION REPORT

Did you complete your mission? How did it go?

December 13, 1545: First day of the Council of Trent, which affirmed dogmas (basic Catholic beliefs) that had been rejected by the Protestants; the council led to reforms within the Catholic Church.

WEDNESDAY, DECEMBER 14

YOUR PRAYER
What do you want to say to God today?

YOUR MISSION

Follow the wisdom of St. John of the Cross: "Learn silence so that God may speak."

YOUR MISSION REPORT
Did you complete your mission? How did it go?

I am the LORD; there is no other

TODAY'S READING
Isaiah 45:6-8, 18, 21-25
God "introduces" himself to King Cyrus of Persia, into whose control the Israelites have fallen. How does God describe himself?

TODAY'S SAINT
St. John of the Cross
(1541-1591)
John of the Cross, together with St. Teresa of Avila, reformed the Carmelite order. He is a Doctor of the Church, well-known for his poetic spiritual writings, include *Ascent of Mount Carmel* and *Dark Night of the Soul*. Some say no other writer has had a greater impact on Catholic spirituality.

"It is best to learn silence so that God may speak."

The Geminid meteor shower (Dec. 13-14) is one of the most brilliant meteor showers, with an average of two meteors crossing the sky every minute.

THURSDAY, DECEMBER 15

My love shall never leave you

TODAY'S READING

Isaiah 54:1-10
Isaiah compares Jerusalem to a woman who is childless, but whom God will now bless with many children. In which lines do you hear God speaking to you?

TODAY'S SAINT

Blessed Mary Frances Schervier (1819-1876)
The founder of the Sisters of the Poor of St. Francis. Besides caring for the sick, the sisters took in prostitutes and helped prisoners find jobs after their release, despite the objections of their supporters. The sisters also tended to the wounded in the U.S. Civil War.

"I felt a glowing flame of holy love for my neighbor."

YOUR PRAYER
What do you want to say to God today?

YOUR MISSION

Even as a young teen, Frances brought food and clothing for the workers at her father's factory, and served in her parish soup kitchen. Your mission: Like Blessed Frances, serve the poor in your neighborhood...or find a way to share in the mission of her order as a friend or volunteer; see sfp-poor.org.

YOUR MISSION REPORT
Did you complete your mission? How did it go?

December 15, 687: Election of Pope Sergius I, who defended Jesus as the Lamb of God and introduced into the liturgy the words: "Lamb of God, you take away the sins of the world, have mercy on us."

FRIDAY, DECEMBER 16

YOUR PRAYER
What do you want to say to God today?

_____
_____
_____
_____

YOUR MISSION

Begin a nine-day Christmas novena for a special intention...perhaps asking Jesus for a special "spiritual gift" for Christmas. You can make up your own nine-day prayer, or search "Christmas novena" online.*

YOUR MISSION REPORT
Did you complete your mission? How did it go?

_____
_____
_____
_____

He testified to the truth

BEGINNING OF CHRISTMAS NOVENAS

Many people pray a special Christmas Novena beginning nine days before Christmas. It is also the beginning of Las Posadas, a re-enactment of Mary and Joseph's search for lodging in Bethlehem.

TODAY'S READING

John 5:33-36

We've heard from John the Baptist quite a bit in the first part of Advent; but now, here is something greater than John. What is it?

TODAY'S SAINT

St. Adelaide of Italy
(931-999)

When her husband, the King of Italy, was poisoned, his enemy had Adelaide locked up in prison. With the help of friends, she escaped through a tunnel and hid in nearby marshes. She sent for help to Otto I, the Holy Roman Emperor; they married, and she became empress. She worked to build up the Church and establish peace between warring kingdoms.

* Bonus mission: Organize your own Las Posadas procession and celebration for your family or parish.

Of her was born Jesus

POPE FRANCIS'S 80TH BIRTHDAY

TODAY'S READING

Matthew 1:1-17
Why are we reading a long list of names today? Matthew wants to show how Jesus is connected to God's saving plan throughout history.

TODAY'S SAINT

St. Olympias (361-408)
The noblewoman who served the Church as a deaconess in Constantinople, using her wealth to build an orphanage and hospital. She was good friends with St. John Chrysostom, and was exiled with him over a religious controversy.

O ANTIPONS BEGIN

Follow them at the bottom of the page, and decode their meaning on page 57.

SATURDAY, DECEMBER 17

YOUR PRAYER

What do you want to say to God today?

YOUR MISSION

In today's Gospel, Matthew reminds his readers of how God has worked to save his people throughout their history. Your mission: Talk to your parents and/or grandparents about how God has worked at key moments in the history of your family. Make a record of their story.

YOUR MISSION REPORT

Did you complete your mission? How did it go?

O Wisdom of our God Most High, guiding creation with power and love: come to teach us the path of knowledge!

SUNDAY, DECEMBER 18

God is with us

YOUR PRAYER
What do you want to say to God today?

YOUR MISSION

As today's readings show, God sends many signs of his desire to be with us. Your mission: Ask your parents to tell the story of your birth...and the signs of God's presence during your birth.

YOUR MISSION REPORT
Did you complete your mission? How did it go?

FOURTH SUNDAY OF ADVENT
Light all four candles on your Advent wreath!

TODAY'S READINGS

Isaiah 7:10-14
Therefore, the Lord himself will give you this sign: the virgin shall conceive, and bear a son, and shall name him Emmanuel.

Romans 1:1-7
Through him we have received the grace of apostleship.

Matthew 1:18-24
"Joseph, son of David, do not be afraid to take Mary your wife into your home."

In the first reading, the prophet Isaiah gives the king a sign of God's desire to save his people. Notice that the Gospel quotes this prophecy to explain the miraculous birth of Jesus. In the second reading, Paul explains the meaning of God's choice to be with us. What words in these readings is God speaking to you?

O Leader of the House of Israel, giver of the Law to Moses on Sinai: come to rescue us with your mighty power!

He will be filled with the Holy Spirit

MONDAY, DECEMBER 19

TODAY'S READINGS

Luke 1:5-25

In today's Gospel we hear the story of the conception of John the Baptist. We hear a very similar story in the first reading, which is about the conception of another great hero of Israel, Samson (see Judges 13:2-7, 24-25). And one of the fathers of Israel, Isaac, was also born to a couple who had no children. Why do you think God chose to bring about the birth of these great heroes in such miraculous ways?

TODAY'S SAINT

Blessed Pope Urban V
(1310-1370)
The humble Benedictine monk and man of the people who, as pope, lived simply and pressed for reform. He worked to curb abuses among the clergy, forbade the harassment or forced conversion of Jews, founded several universities and colleges, and planted vineyards around Rome.

YOUR PRAYER

What do you want to say to God today?

YOUR MISSION

In today's reading, it is Zechariah's turn as a priest to enter the sanctuary of the Temple—that is, the place of God's immediate presence. Your mission: Enter God's immediate presence by receiving the Eucharist or praying before the Eucharist. Listen for the good news God has for you.

YOUR MISSION REPORT

Did you complete your mission? How did it go?

O Root of Jesse's stem, sign of God's love for all his people: come to save us without delay!

TUESDAY, DECEMBER 20

May it be done

YOUR PRAYER
What do you want to say to God today?

YOUR MISSION

Like St. Dominic, pray the Liturgy of the Hours today. Use an app (such as iBreviary or Laudate), or just pray the Canticle of Simeon in the morning, the Angelus at noon, and the Canticle of Mary in the evening (also known as the Magnificat).

YOUR MISSION REPORT
Did you complete your mission? How did it go?

TODAY'S READING
Luke 1:26-38

Here is the story of the Annunciation, in which the angel Gabriel appears to Mary to announce God's plan for her. Read this passage slowly, as if the angel is speaking to you. Which words are especially meaningful to you?

TODAY'S SAINT
St. Dominic of Silos
(1000-1073)

Born to a family of peasants, Dominic was a shepherd before becoming a Benedictine monk. He built a new monastery at Silos, Spain; it became one of the most famous monasteries in the country, known as a place of healing.

GOD'S CREATION
WINTER SOLSTICE

The winter solstice occurs tomorrow, December 21, the day with the fewest hours of sunlight of the year.

O Key of David, opening the gates of God's eternal Kingdom: come and free the prisoners of darkness!

WEDNESDAY, DECEMBER 21

The infant leapt

TODAY'S READING

Luke 1:39-45

Mary goes to visit her relative Elizabeth. Each of these women—one young, one old—shared a special secret: that God was fulfilling the promises he made to his people, and they got to be part of his plan of salvation! Which words in this reading is God using to speak to you?

TODAY'S SAINT

St. Peter Canisius

(1521-1597)

The great Jesuit theologian, Catholic reformer, preacher, and Doctor of the Church who wrote the first Catholic catechism. His fellow Jesuits used to urge him to stop working so hard, to which he said:

"If you have too much to do, with God's help you will find time to do it all."

YOUR PRAYER

What do you want to say to God today?

YOUR MISSION

In today's Gospel, we hear about Mary visiting Elizabeth. Many new people will be visiting Catholic churches this Christmas. Your mission: Make Christmas cards to give to people at church this Christmas, especially people who are new. You might include wrapped candy in some of the cards to give to kids.

YOUR MISSION REPORT

Did you complete your mission? How did it go?

O Radiant Dawn, splendor of eternal light, sun of justice:
come and shine on those who dwell in darkness and in the shadow of death.

THURSDAY, DECEMBER 22

YOUR PRAYER
What do you want to say to God today?

YOUR MISSION

Pray Mary's song of praise, the Magnificat, throughout the day today. See if you can even memorize it! Reflect: How do you make the words of Mary's prayer your own?

YOUR MISSION REPORT
Did you complete your mission? How did it go?

TODAY'S READING
Luke 1:46-56

Today's reading is Mary's biggest speaking part in the Bible, and it is a song of praise, much like the songs of praise of other great women of the Bible. Christians who pray the Divine Office recite or sing this song every evening! What has God done for you that makes you rejoice?

TODAY'S SAINT
Blessed Jacopone da Todi
(d. 1306)

The lawyer who lived a lavish lifestyle until the death of his holy wife. Her death prompted him to give all his possessions to the poor and become a Franciscan penitent, doing penance for his sins in public. His old friends mocked him as "crazy Jim." After many years, he joined a monastery and composed many hymns, including *Stabat Mater*.

"Make me feel as you have felt; make my soul to glow and melt with the love of Christ my Lord."

O King of all nations and keystone of the Church: come and save man, whom you formed from the dust!

FRIDAY, DECEMBER 23

He will be called John

TODAY'S READING

Luke 1:57-66
Jesus' cousin John is born in a wondrous way. He will "prepare the way" for the Messiah, the anointed one of God. How are you preparing for the coming of the Lord at Christmas?

TODAY'S SAINT

St. John Kanty (1390?-1473) A Polish priest and theologian who gave everything he had to God and the poor, keeping only the bare necessities for himself. He even slept on the floor because he didn't have a bed!

"Fight all false opinions, but let your weapons be patience, sweetness and love. Roughness is bad for your own soul and spoils the best cause."

YOUR PRAYER
What do you want to say to God today?

YOUR MISSION

Like John Kanty, give money to the poor in your community or another land. You can send money in time for Christmas by donating online through Catholic Charities, Catholic Relief Services, or another worthy charity.

YOUR MISSION REPORT
Did you complete your mission? How did it go?

O Emmanuel, our King and Giver of Law: come to save us, Lord our God!

SATURDAY, DECEMBER 24

YOUR PRAYER
What do you want to say to God today?

....

....

....

....

YOUR MISSION

On Christmas Eve in the year 1223, St. Francis organized the very first manger scene...with real animals, hay, and possibly even a real baby! Your mission: Create a "live" manger scene, or perform a nativity play, with the help of family and friends.

YOUR MISSION REPORT
Did you complete your mission? How did it go?

....

....

....

....

....

Blessed be the Lord

VIGIL OF THE SOLEMNITY OF THE NATIVITY OF THE LORD

The readings for this morning are different from the readings this evening, because as soon as the sun sets, it's Christmas!

TODAY'S READING

Luke 1:67-79

Zechariah, the father of John the Baptist, offers a song of praise to God at the birth of his son. What is this child's mission going to be, according to his father?

Abraham Hondius, *Annunciation to the Shepherds* (1663)

SUNDAY, DECEMBER 25

Today is born our Savior

SOLEMNITY OF THE NATIVITY OF THE LORD

Merry Christmas! Be sure to say an extra birthday prayer for Jesus this morning!

TODAY'S READINGS

Isaiah 9:1-6
The people who walked in darkness have seen a great light; upon those who dwelt in the land of gloom a light has shone.

Psalm 96
Today is born our Savior, Christ the Lord.

Timothy 2:11-14
The grace of God has appeared, saving all. . . .

Luke 2:1-14
"For today in the city of David a savior has been born for you who is Christ and Lord. And this will be a sign for you: you will find an infant wrapped in swaddling clothes and lying in a manger."

There are four different sets of reading for Christmas, one for each Mass; these readings are from the Mass During the Night.

YOUR PRAYER
What do you want to say to God today?

YOUR MISSION

This Christmas, remember that Jesus was once the same age as you! Your mission: Spend fifteen minutes praying to the child Jesus. Write him a note, if it helps you to concentrate.

YOUR MISSION REPORT
Did you complete your mission? How did it go?

A CHRISTMAS CHECKLIST

DID YOU KNOW THAT CHRISTMAS LASTS EIGHT DAYS? True story—at least for Catholics! The Octave of Christmas lasts from sunset on December 24 through sunset on January 1. But wait, there's more! The Christmas season isn't really over until the Baptism of the Lord, usually two Sundays after January 1 (but not this year!). Ordinary Time (marked with green tabs in this journal) begins the next day.

This is all just to say: Christmas isn't over December 26! Here are some ideas for celebrating the whole Christmas season; check off the ones you plan to do.

- ☐ **Pray before the baby Jesus.** Imitate the shepherds and the wise men by kneeling before the baby Jesus in the Nativity scene at church or home, either after Christmas Mass or on Christmas morning. You could even write a poem for the child Jesus!

- ☐ **Make your own "living manger."** St. Francis created the first manger scene back in 1223 using live animals and people. Enlist the help of your family and friends to re-create a "living Nativity" scene, using whatever you have at hand.

- ☐ **Decorate and bless your Christmas tree.** If your family held off decorating its Christmas tree during Advent, now is the time to decorate it . . . but before you do, bless the tree. Search for "Blessing of a Christmas tree" to find a blessing online.

- ☐ **Bless your home (and bedroom) on Epiphany.** It is traditional to bless your home on the Feast of the Epiphany, maybe because that's when the three kings visited the home of the Holy Family. Search for "Blessing of the Home on Epiphany" online.

- ☐ **Write thank-you notes.** The virtue of gratitude makes you happy—and it makes other people happy to be thanked, too. (Even Santa Claus deserves a thank-you note!) Make it fun by making fancy, decorated notes.

- ☐ **Make a Christmas candle.** Purchase a large white candle, and decorate it with the *chi rho* (the first two letters in the Greek word for Christ) along with the year. Place it in the center of your Advent wreath and light it throughout the Christmas season.

- ☐ **Make Christmas luminaries.** In Spanish-speaking countries and parts of the southwestern United States, it is traditional to set out luminaries—candles set in paper bags weighted with sand—on Christmas Eve. But there is no reason not to make this pretty display anytime during the Christmas season. M:C

Nativity, Master of Vyšší Brod (c. 1350.

Get even more Christmas season ideas at pbgrace.com/celebrate-christmas

MONDAY, DECEMBER 26

Receive my spirit

TODAY'S READING

Acts 6:8-10; 7:54-59
Stephen is arrested and put on trial before the Jewish leaders. The speech he gives makes them so mad, they kill him on the spot.

TODAY'S SAINT

St. Stephen (d. 36)
The deacon who became the first Christian martyr. The Acts of the Apostles says he was one of seven deacons appointed by the Apostles to distribute food and money more fairly to Greek members of the early church. St. Stephen is a martyr "by love, will, and blood": that is, he loved Christ so much, he chose to give up his life for him.

"Lord Jesus, receive my spirit."

YOUR PRAYER
What do you want to say to God today?

YOUR MISSION

Christian martyrs are willing to give up their lives because they believe that the God who gave them life will preserve them in his love. Your mission: Practice being a martyr by giving something up today.

YOUR MISSION REPORT
Did you complete your mission? How did it go?

It's Boxing Day in the UK and Commonwealth countries: Give your servants the day off, and a box of presents!

TUESDAY, DECEMBER 27

What we have seen and heard

YOUR PRAYER
What do you want to say to God today?

TODAY'S READING
1 John 1:1-4
The first letter of St. John the Evangelist opens with him telling us what he has seen and heard. What have you "seen and heard" of God in your life?

TODAY'S SAINT
St. John the Apostle
The apostle who, with his brother James, immediately followed Jesus' call. Five books of the Bible contain his teaching: the Gospel of John, three letters, and the Book of Revelation. St. John was a martyr by love and will: he chose to give his whole life to Jesus, but he died peacefully. He was the only apostle (other than Judas) not to be killed.

"We have come to know and to believe in the love God has for us."

YOUR MISSION

Love of God and others is the main theme of St. John's teaching. Your mission: Tell someone you love them. Better yet, write them a note that also says <u>why</u> you love them.

YOUR MISSION REPORT
Did you complete your mission? How did it go?

December 27, 1983: Pope John Paul II visits Mehmet Ali Ağca in prison and forgives him for shooting and nearly killing him in a 1981 attack in St. Peter's Square.

He ordered the massacre

WEDNESDAY, DECEMBER 28

TODAY'S READING

Matthew 2:13-18
When his plan to track down the Messiah fails, King Herod orders the killing of all the infant boys in Bethlehem in order to destroy the one who threatens his power. Have you ever seen jealousy cause hurt and chaos?

TODAY'S SAINT

Holy Innocents
The children who died in the place of Christ because of King Herod's sin. They are martyrs by blood alone.

CHRISTMAS MARTYRS

On the first three days after Christmas, we remember three types of martyrs, represented by St. Stephen, St. John, and the Holy Innocents. They remind us about the true meaning of Christmas: the Son of God has come to give his whole self to us!

YOUR PRAYER

What do you want to say to God today?

YOUR MISSION

Even today, many innocent children die because of the actions of sinful people. Your mission: Explore ways to help needy children through CARITAS for Children (online: caritas.us), a Catholic organization that teams up with religious orders around the world.

YOUR MISSION REPORT

Did you complete your mission? How did it go?

It's the fourth day of Christmas: Build a Christmas bonfire (with your parents, of course)!

THURSDAY, DECEMBER 29

YOUR PRAYER
What do you want to say to God today?

The glory of your people

TODAY'S READING
Luke 2:22-35

When Jesus' parents present him to God in the Temple, they encounter a man who seems to know a lot about their baby's destiny.

TODAY'S SAINT
St. Thomas Beckett
(1118-1170)

Thomas Beckett was a close advisor to King Henry II, but after being named the Archbishop of Canterbury, he clashed with the king over issues of how much power the king had over the Church. On December 29, 1170, four of the king's knights ambushed the archbishop during evening prayers in Canterbury Cathedral, killing him.

"For the name of Jesus and the protection of the Church, I am ready to embrace death."

YOUR MISSION

It was the angry words of King Henry II that led to Archbishop Beckett's death; the knights who heard the king thought he wanted them to kill the archbishop. It's a good example of how words spoken in anger can cause great harm. Your mission: Keep watch over your tongue to make sure it doesn't harm others.

YOUR MISSION REPORT
Did you complete your mission? How did it go?

King Henry II later did public penance for his role in St. Thomas Beckett's death: the king was scourged at the tomb of the saint.

Rise, take the child

FRIDAY, DECEMBER 30

FEAST OF THE HOLY FAMILY OF JESUS, MARY, AND JOSEPH

On this day, we look to the Holy Family—Joseph, Mary, and Jesus—as a model for how Christian families should live together. According to the Church, the Christian family is a "domestic church"—that is, the Church at home. It is in the family that each member practices love, service, and Christian sacrifice. What has your family taught you?

TODAY'S READING

Matthew 2:13-15, 19-23
Joseph, Mary, and Jesus flee to Egypt to escape persecution.

"Rise, take the child and his mother and go to the land of Israel, for those who sought the child's life are dead."

It's the sixth day of Christmas:
Go sing Christmas carols around your neighborhood!

YOUR PRAYER
What do you want to say to God today?

YOUR MISSION

On this Feast of the Holy Family, tell each person in your family why you're glad they're in your family...and how they have helped you grow spiritually.

YOUR MISSION REPORT
Did you complete your mission? How did it go?

SATURDAY, DECEMBER 31

YOUR PRAYER
What do you want to say to God today?

YOUR MISSION

On this New Year's Eve, think about the biggest events in your life in the past year. How have they changed you? How was God present with you during those events? Use the space on page 107 to record your thoughts.

YOUR MISSION REPORT
Did you complete your mission? How did it go?

The light shines in the darkness

TODAY'S READING
John 1:1-18

Instead of beginning with the story of Jesus' birth, the Gospel of John begins with a story about how Jesus ("the Word," "the light") has been present with God since the very beginning of time. What is your favorite line from this reading?

TODAY'S SAINT

Saint Columba of Sens
(257–273)

Columba was a sixteen-year-old who ran away from home to become a Christian. According to her legend, when she refused to marry the emperor's son, the emperor had her imprisoned. A bear saved her from being attacked by one of the guards. The emperor ordered both her and the bear to be burnt alive, but the bear escaped and rain put out the fire; she was beheaded instead.

New Year's Eve: Stay up until midnight to welcome 2017!

WELCOMING THE NEW YEAR
A TIME FOR REFLECTION

AS THE NEW YEAR APPROACHES, it is traditional for people to remember the biggest events of the past year . . . and to look forward to the year ahead by making resolutions, or firm commitments, about who they want to become. In a way, this tradition resembles the Catholic practice of the daily examen, in which individuals spend time examining their day in order to spy God's presence in its events.

Take some time right now to "examine" the past year in this way, and to look forward to who you want to become in the coming year. M:C

LOOKING BACK AT 2016

Name one "high" and one "low" from 2016—in other words, an event that was really good for you, and one that was really bad. How was God present to you in those events?

LOOKING FORWARD TO 2017

What are your hopes for 2017? What spiritual gifts and virtues do you hope to develop? What bad spiritual habits do you hope to give up? Write a short prayer to God for these intentions.

SUNDAY, JANUARY 1

YOUR PRAYER
What do you want to say to God today?

YOUR MISSION

On this New Year's Day, think about who you want to become in the next year, using the space on page 107 to record your thoughts.*

YOUR MISSION REPORT
Did you complete your mission? How did it go?

Mary kept all these things in her heart

SOLEMNITY OF MARY, THE HOLY MOTHER OF GOD

This is the "octave," or eighth, day of Christmas. On this day, we remember that Mary is not only the mother of the child Jesus, but that this child is divine—God come to us in human flesh. Because we believe Jesus is God, we can call Mary the "mother of God."

TODAY'S READING

Numbers 6:22-27
The LORD bless you and keep you! The LORD let his face shine upon you, and be gracious to you! The LORD look upon you kindly and give you peace!

Galatians 4:4-7
God sent the spirit of his Son into our hearts, crying out, "Abba, Father!"

Luke 2:16-19
And Mary kept all these things, reflecting on them in her heart.

---

* Bonus mission: On this World Day of Peace, look up the pope's message of peace to the whole world. Search online for "World Day of Peace" and "pope."

MONDAY, JANUARY 2

Make straight the way of the Lord

TODAY'S READING

John 1:19-28

Who is John the Baptist? The religious leaders in Jerusalem want to know. His answer is not what they expected! How do *you* answer that question?

TODAY'S SAINT

Zdislava Berka (1220–1252)

Zdislava ran away from home at the age of seven to become a hermit in the woods, but was caught. Later, she was forced to marry a count. She had four children, attended Mass regularly, and while her husband was away at war, she opened up their fortified castle to refugees. The count didn't always like her generosity; when he chased a sick man out of his bed, Zdlislava sold the bed and put a crucifix in its place. The count never complained again!

YOUR PRAYER

What do you want to say to God today?

YOUR MISSION

"Who are you?... What do you have to say for yourself?" John answered that question by telling them the mission God had given him. Your mission: Come up with an answer to that question for yourself, one that reflects who you are in relation to God. Write it down in your mission report at the end of the day.

YOUR MISSION REPORT

Did you complete your mission? How did it go?

Today is also the feast day of St. Basil the Great (330-379), a Greek bishop who fought heresy, cared for the poor, and helped found Eastern communal monasticism.

TUESDAY, JANUARY 3

Behold, the Lamb of God

YOUR PRAYER
What do you want to say to God today?

TODAY'S READING
John 1:29-34

John the Baptist is loud and clear about who Jesus is: the Son of God. How does John know this?

TODAY'S SAINT

Blessed Marie Anne Blondin
(1809-1899)

Blessed Marie Anne founded an order of nuns, the Sisters of St. Anne, to provide schools to French-speaking children in rural Canada. The order was successful, but politics resulted in her being removed as superior. She spent the rest of her life doing laundry for her order, a situation she humbly accepted, saying:

"The deeper a tree sinks its roots into the soil, the greater are its chances of growing and producing fruit."

YOUR MISSION

Spend 10 minutes doing an imagination prayer. Imagine you are in the Jordan river, witnessing the encounter between Jesus and John. What does it look like? What do you hear and see and feel? What do you want to ask John, afterward? Record these insights in your mission report and ask Jesus in prayer to meet him someday, like John the Baptist did.

YOUR MISSION REPORT
Did you complete your mission? How did it go?

Today is the annual Festival of Sleep day: Spend extra time in your pajamas!

WEDNESDAY, JANUARY 4

Come and you will see

TODAY'S READINGS

John 1:35-42

Jesus invites his first followers to "come and see" where he is staying, thus launching their lives in a completely new direction. How would you answer Jesus' question: "What are you looking for?"

TODAY'S SAINT

St. Elizabeth Ann Seton
(1774-1821)

Elizabeth grew up in high society in New York City, but when her wealthy husband died, she completely changed her life. She joined the Catholic Church, which led to her rejection by friends and family. After taking care of her children, she began a new religious order that started the first Catholic schools in the U.S.

"Cheerfulness prepares a glorious mind for all the noblest acts."

YOUR PRAYER

What do you want to say to God today?

YOUR MISSION

Before becoming Catholic, Elizabeth prayed hard and listed her reasons for converting.* Your mission: At the end of today, list your reasons for being Catholic in your mission report.

YOUR MISSION REPORT

Did you complete your mission? How did it go?

---

* Elizabeth had three reasons for becoming Catholic: 1. Jesus' real, physical presence in the Eucharist. 2. Devotion to Mary. 3. The Catholic Church's direct, historical connection to Jesus and the apostles.

THURSDAY, JANUARY 5

YOUR PRAYER
What do you want to say to God today?

YOUR MISSION

Jesus used humor to make points and to connect with people, like when he teases Nathaniel in today's reading. Your mission: Use humor to make a positive connection with someone today.

YOUR MISSION REPORT
Did you complete your mission? How did it go?

Can anything good come from Nazareth?

TODAY'S READING

John 1:43-51

Jesus continues to call his disciples, this time Philip and Nathaniel, who at first mocks Jesus for coming from the little village of Nazareth. But minutes later, he declares Jesus the Son of God! What happened?

TODAY'S SAINT

St. John Neumann
(1811-1860)

John came to the United States from Bohemia in 1836 to minister to immigrant Catholics. He eventually became the bishop of Philadelphia and began a network of Catholic schools.

"Everyone who breathes has a mission, has a work. God sees every one of us; He creates every soul, . . . for a purpose. He deigns to need every one of us. As Christ has His work, we too have ours; as He rejoiced to do His work, we must rejoice in ours also."

It's the 12th day of Christmas—time to celebrate Twelfth Night with traditions like a yule log and eating King Cake!

The Son of God gives us life

FRIDAY, JANUARY 6

TODAY'S READING

1 John 5:5-13

Jesus is the Son of God! We have heard this proclaimed many times this week. Why is it so important to know that Jesus is the Son of God?

TODAY'S SAINT

St. Gertrude of Delft
(d. 1358)
After her fiancé left her to marry another, Gertrude was so heartbroken, she couldn't work. Eventually she joined a community of Beguines, lay women (not nuns) who devoted themselves to prayer, Scripture, and charity. She counseled others in spiritual matters, "reading" their souls and sometimes predicting the future; she even received the five marks of Jesus' wounds on the cross, the stigmata. Her dying words were:

"I am longing to go home."

YOUR PRAYER
What do you want to say to God today?

YOUR MISSION

Gertrude was devastated when her fiancé left her—especially since the other woman had been unfair to her. But after a while, inspired by the love of God, she began going out of her way to treat the other woman kindly. Your mission: Like Gertrude, pray for God's help to always forgive those who hurt you.

YOUR MISSION REPORT
Did you complete your mission? How did it go?

January 6, 1412: St. Joan of Arc is born; inspired by a vision, she led the French army to victory.

SATURDAY, JANUARY 7

Do whatever he tells you

YOUR PRAYER
What do you want to say to God today?

TODAY'S READING
John 2:1-11

Jesus' first miracle is supplying wine for a wedding party. Can you think of other times that Jesus talks about wedding feasts? What is another time he offers people wine?

TODAY'S SAINT
St. André Bessette
(1845-1937)

André tried many jobs before finding the perfect fit as the doorman at Notre Dame College in Montreal. There, he welcomed people, listened to their problems, and prayed for them. He became so well known for curing people of sickness that thousands of pilgrims flocked to his door.

"It is with the smallest brushes that the artist paints the most exquisitely beautiful pictures."

YOUR MISSION

Brother André became so popular, he received 80,000 letters a year! People sought him because of his reputation of curing diseases, but he was also a good listener. Your mission: Practice really listening to someone today.

YOUR MISSION REPORT
Did you complete your mission? How did it go?

January 7th is Old Rock Day: Start a collection of old rocks!

We have seen his star

SUNDAY, JANUARY 8

THE EPIPHANY OF THE LORD

An *epiphany* is a sudden discovery or revelation. Today we celebrate the revelation of the Son of God not only to his chosen people, but to all the nations.

TODAY'S READINGS

Isaiah 60:1-6
. . . but upon you the LORD shines, and over you appears his glory. Nations shall walk by your light, and kings by your shining radiance.

Ephesians 3:2-3a, 5-6
The Gentiles are coheirs, members of the same body, and copartners in the promise in Christ Jesus through the gospel.

Matthew 2:1-12
The magi were overjoyed at seeing the star, and on entering the house they saw the child with Mary his mother.

YOUR PRAYER
What do you want to say to God today?

YOUR MISSION

On the Feast of Epiphany, we are reminded that Christ came for people of all nations. Your mission: Find out who has moved to your community from another nation recently. (Contact your school district, parish, or Catholic Charities.) Make them a welcome basket and bring it to their new home sometime this month.*

YOUR MISSION REPORT
Did you complete your mission? How did it go?

---

* Bonus mission: National Migration Week begins: Search "National Migration Week" for ways to help from the U.S. Catholic bishops.

MONDAY, JANUARY 9

YOUR PRAYER
What do you want to say to God today?

YOUR MISSION

Did you know that at your baptism, you received the power to continue Christ's work in the world as priest, prophet, and king? Your mission: On this Feast of the Baptism of the Lord, ask your parents to tell you about your own baptism. If you can, locate your baptismal gown, certificate, and candle.

YOUR MISSION REPORT
Did you complete your mission? How did it go?

The heavens were opened

THE BAPTISM OF THE LORD

The Feast of the Baptism of the Lord recalls the baptism of Jesus by John the Baptist—and reminds us of our own baptisms.

TODAY'S READING

Matthew 3:13-17

Did you know that *you* are a beloved child of God, too?

TODAY'S SAINT

St. Angela of Foligno
(1248-1309)

After she lost her husband and three sons in the plague, Angela went on a pilgrimage to Assisi; overwhelmed by the love of God, she gave away all her wealth and vowed to live by the rule of St. Francis. She wrote down her mystical visions of God's love, and served the poor and sick.

"In an excess of wonder, I cried out, 'The world is pregnant with God!' . . . I understood how small is the whole of creation . . . but the power of God fills it all to overflowing."

The Christmas season ends today: Time to take down your Christmas decorations!

SPECIAL MISSION: DECODE AN ANCIENT HYMN

THE O ANTIPHONS are an ancient liturgical *antiphon* (response) sung or recited during the last seven days of Advent (one each day from December 17 through December 23) as part of the Liturgy of Hours. (The Liturgy of Hours is the way the Church prays throughout the day.)

No one knows the exact origin of the O Antiphons, but Christians have been singing them since at least the fifth century. You might recognize some of the words, because the O Antiphons are the basis of the popular hymn *O Come, O Come Emmanuel*.

Each antiphon begins with a title of Christ taken from the Old Testament. Do a little detective work to figure out what they mean, using the Scripture references as clues.

Wisdom
Isaiah 11:2-3
Isaiah 28:29

O Wisdom, coming forth from the mouth of the Most High,
reaching from one end to the other,
mightily and sweetly ordering all things:
Come and teach us the way of prudence.

Adonai
Isaiah 11:4-5
Isaiah 33:22

O Adonai, and leader of the House of Israel,
who appeared to Moses in the fire of the burning bush
and gave him the law on Sinai:
Come and redeem us with an outstretched arm.

Root
Isaiah 11:1
Isaiah 11:10

O Root of Jesse, standing as a sign among the peoples;
before you kings will shut their mouths,
to you the nations will make their prayer:
Come and deliver us, and delay no longer.

Key of David
Isaiah 22:22
Isaiah 9:7
Isaiah 42:7

O Key of David and sceptre of the House of Israel;
you open and no one can shut;
you shut and no one can open:
Come and lead the prisoners from the prison house,

Morning star
Isaiah 9:2

O Morning Star,
splendor of light eternal and sun of righteousness:
Come and enlighten those who dwell in darkness and the shadow of death.

King of Nations
Isaiah 2:4
Isaiah 28:16

O King of the nations, and their desire,
the cornerstone making both one:
Come and save the human race,
which you fashioned from clay.

Emmanuel
Isaiah 7:14

O Emmanuel, our king and our lawgiver,
the hope of the nations and their Saviour:
Come and save us, O Lord our God.

BONUS
Some people say that the first letter in each Latin title, working backwards from the last antiphon, spells out a secret message in Latin. Can you figure it out?

Sapientia Adonai Radix Clavis Oriens Rex Emmanuel

ERO CRAS = "Tomorrow I come"

EXTRA MISSIONS

Choose any of these missions as a substitute for your daily mission, or as an extra bonus mission. You can check off the ones you complete.

PRAYER MISSIONS

- ☐ Pray the Liturgy of the Hours
- ☐ Attend daily Mass
- ☐ Spend five minutes in silent prayer
- ☐ Pray for someone annoying
- ☐ Bless someone
- ☐ Make an examination of conscience and receive the sacrament of Penance and Reconciliation
- ☐ Memorize a cool prayer no one else knows
- ☐ Lead grace before a meal—with flair

SERVICE MISSIONS

- ☐ Give away some of your stuff
- ☐ Visit an elderly person (bring a gift)
- ☐ Ask God to show you someone who needs your help . . . then help them
- ☐ Do a chore (like cleaning the kitchen or sweeping the floor) . . . in secret
- ☐ Tip a fast food worker
- ☐ Secretly pay for someone else's meal/drink/snack at a store or restaurant
- ☐ Leave a positive comment with someone's boss
- ☐ Leave encouraging notes all around
- ☐ Listen to someone who is having problems

TRAINING MISSIONS

- ☐ Forgive someone who hurt you
- ☐ Be cheerful
- ☐ Offer up physical pain to God
- ☐ List ten things you can be thankful for today
- ☐ Admit you were wrong and ask for forgiveness
- ☐ Don't argue all day
- ☐ Learn more about the saint of the day (in a book or online)

CHALLENGE MISSIONS

- ☐ Write your spiritual autobiography (page 141)
- ☐ Do Eucharistic adoration for an hour
- ☐ Spend half an hour in quiet prayer
- ☐ Fast for a special prayer intention
- ☐ Go without screens for 48 hours
- ☐ Face your greatest fear (pray first!)
- ☐ Read a book of the Bible you haven't read before
- ☐ Start a club for kids like you who want to serve God
- ☐ Write thank-you notes to your parents and grandparents
- ☐ Love your enemy

THE MISSION CONTINUES...

COMING UP

LENT AND EASTER

Volume 3: February 2017 to May 2017

ORDINARY TIME

Volume 4: June 2017 to September 2017

Purchase them at www.gracewatch.media/mission.
Your journals will arrive approximately one month before the cover date.

If you have any questions or suggestions,
please contact us at mission@gracewatch.org.

MISSION:CHRISTIAN

Advent+Christmastide 2016

Conceptual design and editorial development by Jerry Windley-Daoust
Editorial contributions by Jennifer Shlameuss-Perry and Susan Windley-Daoust
Visual design and build by Steve Nagel
Original art for "Meet the Saints" feature by Carly Lobenhofer

MISSION:CHRISTIAN BOOKS

Copyright © 2016 by Gracewatch Media. All rights reserved. No part of this book may be reproduced by any means without the written permission of the publisher.
ISBN: 9781944008253

Acknowledgments

Scripture texts in this work are taken from the New American Bible, revised edition © 2010, 1991, 1986, 1970 Confraternity of Christian Doctrine, Washington, D.C. and are used by permission of the copyright owner. All Rights Reserved. No part of the New American Bible may be reproduced in any form without permission in writing from the copyright owner.

The artwork on pages 5, 39, 73, and 109 are copyrighted by Carly Lobenhofer.

The artwork on the cover is The Nativity, a tapestry by Jan van Roome (1520) located in the Museum of Applied Arts, Budapest.

The images of saints throughout this book are taken from Wikimedia Commons and are in the public domain.

"A Mission Prayer" on page 5 is adapted from a meditation by John Henry Newman:
"Hope in God—Creator," March 7, 1848, in *Meditations and Devotions*.

www.ingramcontent.com/pod-product-compliance
Lightning Source LLC
Chambersburg PA
CBHW081339080526
44588CB00017B/2683